The 'an' Van

By Viola & Zaida Stefano

VeeZee Publications

Copyright © VeeZee Publications Pty. Ltd. 2024
First published in Australia in 2024
by VeeZee Publications Pty. Ltd.
veezeepublications.com

The right of Viola Stefano to be identified as the author of this work have been asserted by her in accordance with the **Copyright Amendment (Moral Rights) Act 2000.**

All rights reserved. Apart from any use as permitted by the author & under the **Copyright Act 1968**, no part may be reproduced, copied, scanned, stored in a retrieval system, recorded, or shared, by any means or in any form, without prior written & signed authorization from the publisher.

ISBN: 978-1-923120-08-2

A catalogue record of this book is available from the **National Library of Australia.**

Author: Viola Stefano
Illustrations, cover & internal designs: Zaida Stefano

Illustrations copyright © Zaida Stefano 2024
Design copyright © Zaida Stefano 2024

Disclaimer: The content presented in this book is meant for educational purposes only. The author & publisher claim no accountability to any entity or person for any liability, damage, or loss caused or assumed to be caused directly or indirectly as a consequence of the application, use, or interpretation of the material in this book.

Core words used in this book

I	want	**can**	**stop**	**look**
like	more	**he**	go	**see**
here	**what**	do	**the**	**and**
out	where	**we**	it	**up**
not	**they**	when	**that**	**down**
she	**now**	**them**	**is**	put
help	off	you	yes	on
turn	who	**this**	no	why
done	make	**a**	**to**	under
come	**in**	some	which	**there**
open	**get**	good	same	home

Look. Nan and Fran can see a van.

Dan the man sat in the van.

Dan can see Nan and Fran.

Nan and Fran can see Dan the man.

Stop Dan. What is in that big red van?

Nan and Fran ran to the van.

They are hot now but Dan has a plan for them.

He taps the big tan seat.

Come! Get up into the van now, Nan and Fran.

Sit down there next to Jan, my gran.

We can cool down and nap here at this little blue fan.

Words that end in 'an' in this book

Nan	Fran	Dan
Jan	ran	can
plan	fan	gran
van	man	tan

Words with a short 'a' sound in this book

sat	has	taps
that	at	nap
	and	

Learning made easy with VeeZee

VeeZee Publications

Wait, there's more!

Visit our website for information about our range of readers & supporting products.

veezeepublications.com

www.ingramcontent.com/pod-product-compliance
Lightning Source LLC
Chambersburg PA
CBHW042107090526
44590CB00004B/122